Workbook

BACKPACK 2

Second Edition

Mario Herrera · Diane Pinkley

PEARSON
Longman

Backpack 2, Second Edition
Workbook

Pearson Education, 10 Bank Street, White Plains, NY 10606, USA

Staff credits: The people who made up the *Backpack 2* Workbook team, representing editorial, production, design, and manufacturing, are Rhea Banker, Carol Brown, Sarah Bupp, Tracey Cataldo, Gina DiLillo, Christine Edmonds, Ed Lamprich, Maria Pia Marrella, Linda Moser, Leslie Patterson, Diane Pinkley, Edie Pullman, Susan Saslow, Loretta Steeves, and Andrew Vaccaro.
Text composition: TSI Graphics
Text font: 14 pt HSP Helvetica Text
Illustration credits: Aubrey, Meg, 55, 56, 87; Berlin, Rose Mary, 26, 65, 78, 88; Bowser, Ken, 9, 12, 14, 34, 36; Boyer, Robin, 72; Bridy, Dan, 4, 16, 24, 33, 36; Briseno, Luis, 11, 18, 30, 44, 66, 73; Catanese, Donna, 8, 38, 41, 58, 82, 84; Cleyet-Merle, Laurence, 7; Davis, Billy, 2; Dillard, Sarah, 28, 86; Durrel, Julie, 1, 3; Flanagan, Kate, 6, 18, 34, 43, 46, 54, 81; Klug, Dave, 34, 52, 53; Miranda, Hugo, 7, 31, 61, 91–108; Newman, Fran, 23, 53; Pye, Trevor, 31, 32, 61, 62, 63, 64, 78; Sexton, Brenda, 71; Smith, Jaime, 42, 44, 48
Photo credits: l = left, c = center, r = right, t = top, b = bottom;
Page 22 (t) © Rudi Von Briel/PhotoEdit, Inc., (b) © PhotoDisc, Inc;
37 (tl) © James Davis/Eye Ubiquitous/Corbis, (tr) © Corbis,
(bl) © Kevin R. Morris/Bohemian Nomad Picturemakers/Corbis,
(br) © Robert Essel NYC/Corbis; 43 © Christopher Cormack/Corbis;
74 (bl) © Randy Green/Taxi/Getty Images, (bc) © Martin Harvey;
Gallo Images/Corbis, (br) © MetaTools

ISBN-13: 978-0-13-245130-7
ISBN-10: 0-13-245130-1

PEARSON LONGMAN ON THE WEB

Pearsonlongman.com offers online resources for teachers and students. Access our Companion Websites, our online catalog, and our local offices around the world.

Visit us at **pearsonlongman.com**.

Printed in the United States of America
20 18

Contents

1 First Day of Class

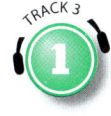

TRACK 3

1 Listen. Draw lines to match. Color pictures to match.

Time for School!

I have a blue pencil.

I have a red pen.

I have a green backpack.

School time again!

I have pink erasers.

I have glue and tape.

I have a white ruler.

School time is great!

I have purple notebooks.

My markers are cool.

They go in my backpack.

Let's walk to school.

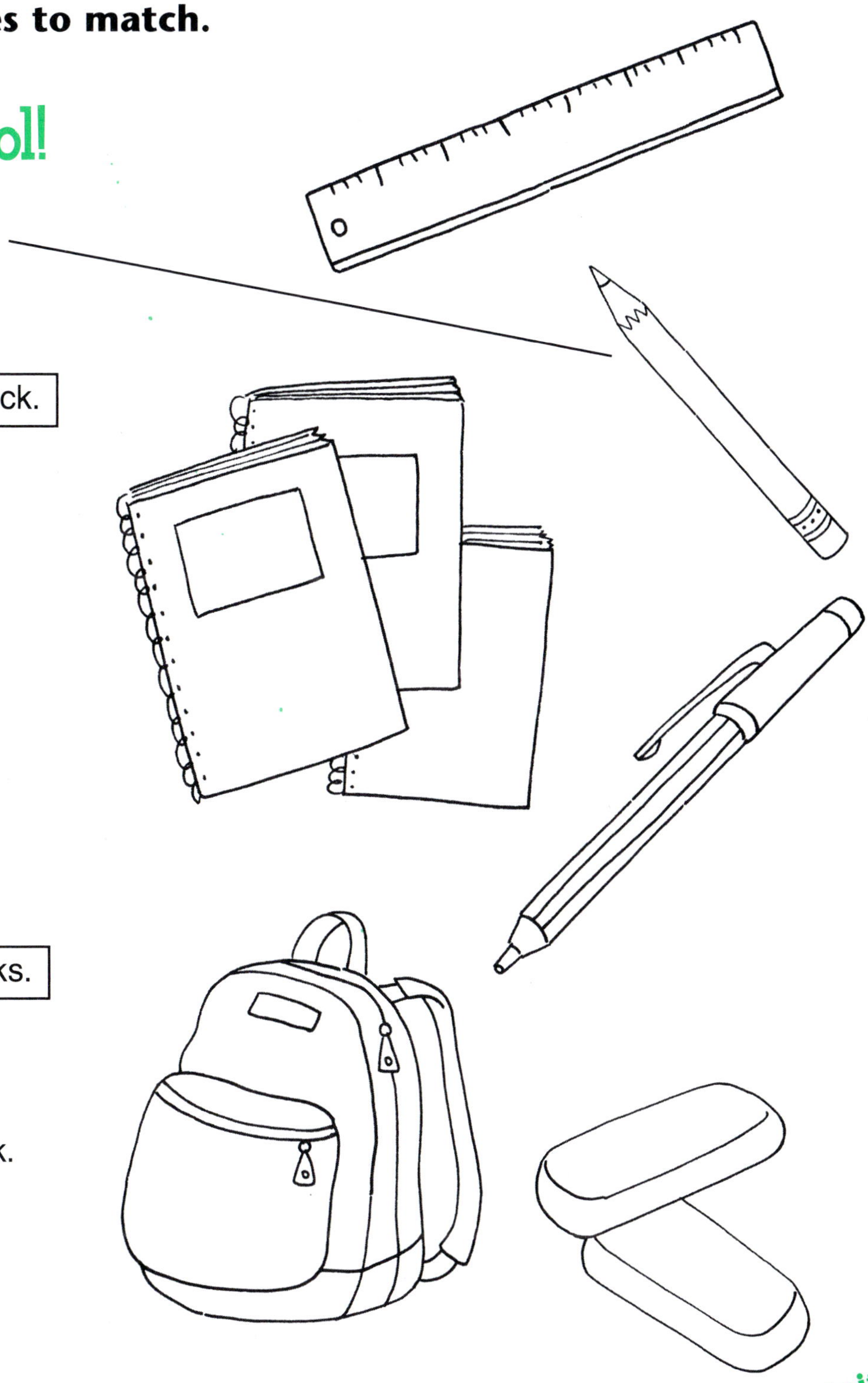

2 Match. Write. Use words from the box.

11 eleven	12 twelve	14 fourteen
16 sixteen	18 eighteen	20 twenty

1. There are _____twelve_____ stickers.

2. There are _____ markers.

3. There are _____ crayons.

4. There are _____ pencils.

5. There are _____ pens.

6. There are _____ erasers.

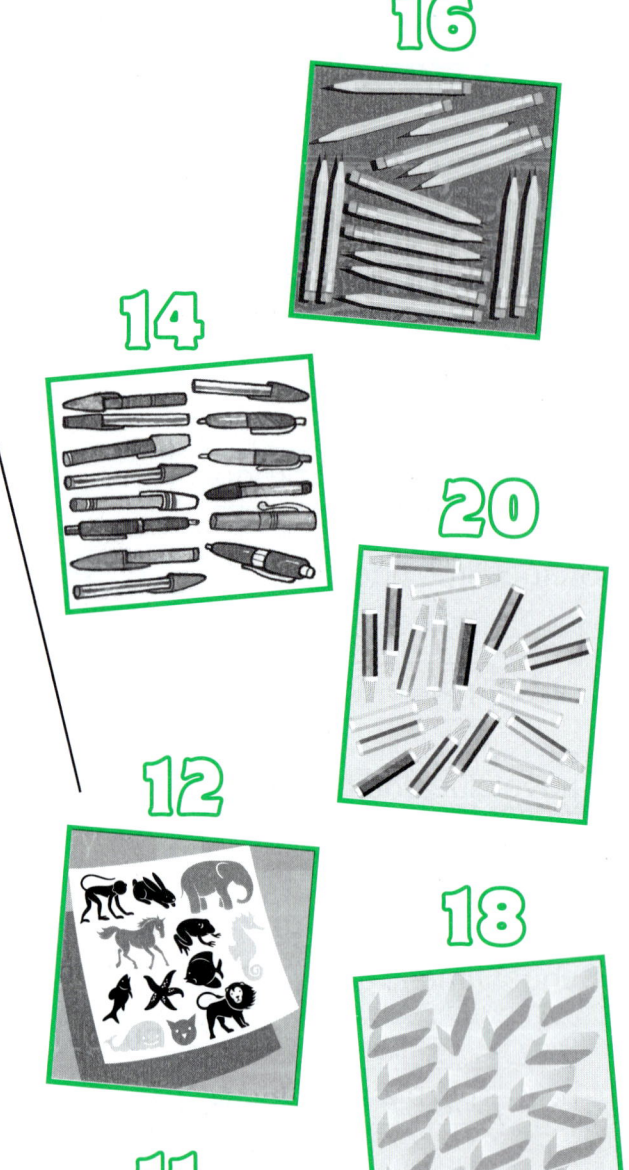

Grammar

She's He's They're	walking to the door.	she's = she is he's = he is they're = they are

 Look. Write *She's*, *He's*, or *They're*.

1. _____ gluing shapes.

2. _____ listening to a story.

3. _____ cutting paper.

 Write. Use words from the box.   singing   talking   walking

1. They're _____.   2. He's _____.   3. She's _____.

5 **Write.**

1. What is he doing?

   _He's reading_____ a book.

2. What is she doing?

   _____

3. What are they doing?

   _____

6 **Write *There is* or *There are*. Draw.**

_____ one ball.   _____ seven crayons.

4

Find the words and circle them.

g	w	a	s	o	e	c	y	b	z	d
k	c	o	u	n	t	i	n	g	f	s
v	o	j	h	r	a	n	d	i	l	c
a	l	x	q	p	z	t	t	j	r	t
b	o	p	e	n	i	n	g	i	k	a
b	r	o	m	b	x	a	w	y	p	l
s	i	t	t	i	n	g	l	u	n	k
u	n	b	q	c	y	m	u	r	q	i
z	g	u	e	k	s	p	b	c	x	n
w	b	w	h	r	e	a	d	i	n	g

coloring
counting
opening
reading
sitting
talking

 Write. Draw and color.

Draw two friends on the playground. What are they doing?

They're _____.

1. _____ crayons.

2. _____ notebooks.

3. She's _____.

4. He's _____.

5. They're _____.

TRACK 5

10 **Listen. Write. Match.**

School Is Cool!

I am cutting, I am gluing,

    I am _____, too.

I like school. School is cool!

He is reading, he is writing,

    he is _____, too.

He likes school. School is cool!

She is talking, she is playing,

    she is _____, too.

She likes school. School is cool!

The Magic Backpack

11 **Read** *The Magic Backpack*. **Write** *yes* **or** *no*.

1. There are sixteen purple paper clips.   *yes*

2. There are three yellow pencils.   _____

3. There are five white rulers.   _____

4. There are fourteen pink erasers.   _____

5. There are nine green pens.   _____

6. There are twelve stickers.   _____

7. There are eleven red markers.   _____

8. There is one magic backpack.   _____

12 **What is in** *your* **backpack? Write how many.**

There is one apple in my backpack.

_____

_____

_____

_____

_____

_____

Work with a partner. Tell what's in your backpack.

Review

 Look. Circle a sentence.

1. She's cutting paper.

   (She's coloring pictures.)

2. They're talking.

   They're counting.

3. He's writing a story.

   He's listening to a story.

 Look. Write a sentence.

1. _____

   _____

2. _____

   _____

3. _____

   _____

 What are you doing? Write a sentence.

_____

_____

Cut-out Activity ✂ - - - - - - - - - - - - -

A. Count. Write the number and the number word.

B. Find a partner. Cut out the cards. Talk about *How many.*

How many boxes are there?

There are eleven boxes.

_____ boxes

_____ stars

_____ pencils

_____ apples

_____ planes

_____ books

_____ squares

_____ triangles

_____ bikes

_____ cars

Students write numerals and number words. Then they cut out their cards and play a memory game with a partner. Both students' cards are mixed up and placed facedown. Student 1 turns over two cards. Student 2 asks *How many?* Student 1 tells how many are on each card. Students keep the pairs they find. They continue until all pairs are found.

Fun and Games

TRACK 6

1 **Listen and write. Draw lines to match.**

Hide and Seek

I close my eyes and my friends run!
Ready or not, here I come.

Where is Lucy? Now I see!

She's _____ the swing, next to Dee.

Where is Peter? Now I see!

He's high up there _____ the tree.

I close my eyes and my friends run!
Ready or not, here I come.

Where is Alice? Now I see!

She's _____ the bush, in front of me.

Where are you? Now I see!
You're right here, looking at me.

I close my eyes and my friends run!
Ready or not, here I come.

behind

under

in

2 **Write. Use words from the box.**

behind	between	in	in front of	on	under

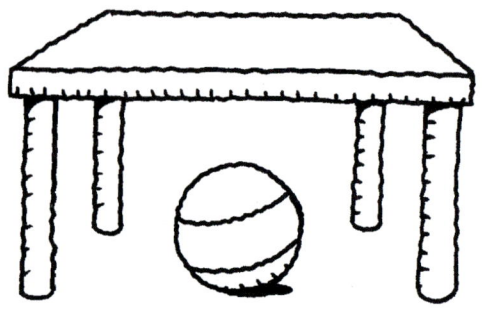

1. The ball is _____ the table.

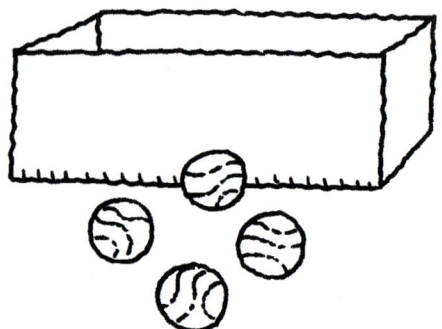

2. The marbles are _____ the box.

3. The dog is _____ the tree and the bush.

4. The kite is _____ the tree.

5. The backpack is _____ the chair.

6. The cat is _____ the backpack.

| He She | **likes** to play baseball. |
| I They | **like** to play baseball. |

3 **Write *like* or *likes*.**

1. They _____ to play checkers.

2. He _____ to fly kites.

3. She _____ to climb trees.

4. They _____ to play hide and seek.

5. I _____ to jump rope.

6. She _____ to skate.

4 **Look. Draw lines to match.**
Write the answers.

1. What does she like to do?

   _____

play checkers

2. What does he like to do?

   _____

jump rope

3. What do they like to do?

   _____

ride a bike

5 Count and write the word that tells how many.

| 10 ten | 20 twenty | 30 thirty | 40 forty | 50 fifty | 60 sixty |

_____ checkers

_____ dominoes

_____ marbles

_____ cards

6 Write the word for the number. Draw.

There are 10 checkers.

There are _____ checkers.

There are 20 marbles.

There are _____ marbles.

14

**Write. Use words from the box.**

ball	
bike	
checkers	
kite	
tree	

1. I like to fly a _____.
2. I like to catch and throw a _____.
3. I like to play _____ with my friends.
4. I like to climb a _____ in the park.
5. I like to ride a _____.

8 **What do you like to do? Draw and color. Write.**

I like to _____.

 **Listen and write.**

1. His baseball bat is _____ his bed.

2. Her notebook is _____ her backpack.

3. Their bikes are _____ the tree.

 **Listen. Draw lines to match.**

Having Fun

I like to fly my kite in the sky.
I'm not the only one.
My friends like to fly kites in the sky.
We are having fun!

I like to ride my bike in the park.
I'm not the only one.
My friends like to ride bikes in the park.
We are having fun!

I like to throw a ball in the air.
I'm not the only one.
My friends like to throw balls in the air.
We are having fun!

11 Write your own verse. Draw a picture.

I like to _____ my _____

    in the _____.

I'm not the only one.

My friends like to _____

    in the _____.

We are having fun!

Playing Games

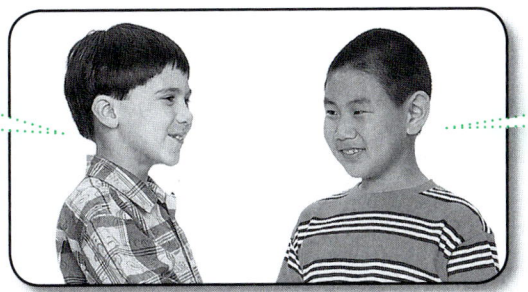

What do they like to do?

They like to throw balls.

 Read *Playing Games*. Write. Check (✔) the boxes.

 1   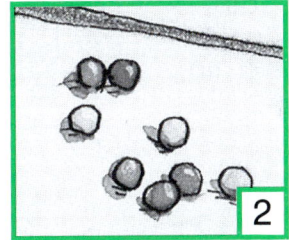 2    3    4

What do they like to do?	balls	cards	chalk	marbles
1. Children from Colombia like to throw __balls__.	✔			
2. Children from Indonesia like to shoot _____.				
3. Children from Mexico like to play a game with _____.				
4. Children from Taiwan like to turn over _____.				

13 **Where are you from? What do children from your country like to play? Write.**

I am from _____.

Children from _____ like to play _____.

Review

14 **Count and write.**

1. There are _____20_____ checkers in front of the table.

2. There are _____ checkers on the table.

3. There are _____ checkers next to the snake.

4. There are _____ checkers between the snake and the giraffe.

5. There are _____ circles on the train.

6. There are _____ squares on the train.

15 **Write the word.**
Draw lines to match.

1. They like to _____play_____ checkers.

2. She likes to _____ her bike.

3. He likes to _____ trees.

4. They like to _____ kites.

5. She likes to _____ marbles.

ride

play

fly

shoot

climb

18

Cut-out Activity ✂ - - - - - - - - - - - - - - -

A. Draw pictures.
  Cut out the cards.
B. Find a partner.
  Talk about where things are.

Where is the bat?

The bat is next to the balls.

behind	between	in front of	next to	on

a backpack	a bat	a cat	a jump rope
a kite	three worms	two balls	two birds

Students draw pictures of the objects on the cards. Students work with a partner to talk about the location of the objects as they place them **behind, between, in front of, next to,** and **on** each other. When talking about more than one object, students ask **Where are. . .?**

3 Our New House

TRACK 9

1 Listen and write. Use words from the box.

aunt	brother	cousins	family	father
grandfather	grandmother	mother	uncle	

My Family

Don't be shy—come talk to me.

Meet the people in my _____!

Here's my _____, my sister

and _____.

That little baby's my new _____!

Come say hello to my _____ Lou,

_____ Sally, and my

_____, too!

Over there is my _____ Jill.

That tall man is my _____ Bill.

Don't be shy—come talk to me.

Meet the people in my family!

Unit 3

21

2 **Write. Use words from the box. Draw.**

| aunt | cousins | grandfather | grandmother | uncle |

1. These are my aunt's children.

   They are my _____.

2. This is my mother's mother.

   She is my _____.

3. This is my mother's sister.

   She is my _____.

4. This is my mother's brother.

   He is my _____.

5. This is my mother's father.

   He is my _____.

6. And this is ME!

Where's your mother?	**She's** in the living room.	where's = where is
		he's/she's = he is/she is
Where's your sink?	**It's** in the kitchen.	it's = it is
Where are your cousins?	**They're** in the kitchen.	they're = they are

 **Write.**

1. Where's your brother?

_____ in the dining room.

2. Where are your mother and father?

_____ in the living room.

3. Where's Aunt Ella?

_____ in the bedroom.

4. Where's the refrigerator?

_____ in the kitchen.

 Where's your mirror? Write.

_____

_____

5 **Write Where's or Where are.**

1. _____ the lamp?

2. _____ the plants?

3. _____ the curtains?

4. _____ the mirror?

5. _____ the shelves?

6 **Find and color. Ask a friend where these things are in a house.**

chair	lamp	rug
stove	tub	TV

Find the words and circle them.

m	t	k	i	t	c	h	e	n	w	s
y	b	a	t	c	e	o	m	m	i	r
v	a	c	h	l	u	t	i	p	k	h
e	t	w	t	u	g	r	m	k	s	t
c	h	a	i	r	a	d	i	j	t	w
o	r	p	a	b	e	d	r	o	o	m
y	o	t	w	t	u	g	r	u	o	g
o	o	n	a	d	h	j	o	k	t	u
e	m	w	t	u	g	r	r	o	s	t

bathroom

bedroom

chair

kitchen

mirror

8 **What's your favorite room? What's in it?**
Write. Draw and color.

I like my _____.

In this room, there's a _____ and a _____.

9 Listen and circle.

TRACK 10

1. Ramona's desk is **behind** / **under** the window.

2. Her **computer** / **notebook** is on her desk.

3. There's a **chair** / **night table** next to her bed.

4. Her night table has a **clock** / **radio** on it.

5. Her bedroom is mostly **blue and green** / **pink and white**.

10 Listen and write. Color to match.
TRACK 11

What Color Is Your Bedroom?

Joe's bedroom is all in _____—
    his rug and his mirror,
    and his clock and bed!

Sue's bedroom is all in _____—
    her dresser and her phone,
    and her answering machine!

My bedroom is all in _____—
    my lamp and my curtains,
    and my computer, too!

11 What colors are in your bedroom? Write.

_____

_____

_____

_____

I have a blue
desk and a
white chair.

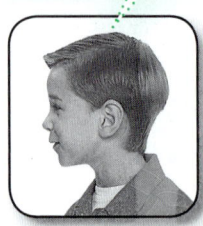

26

Moving Day

 Read *Moving Day.* **Circle** *yes* **or** *no.*

Rooms in Sonia's New House		
computer room	yes	no
dining room	yes	no
kitchen	yes	no
living room	yes	no
playroom	yes	no
three bedrooms	yes	no

Things in Sonia's New Bedroom		
bed	yes	no
chair	yes	no
lamp	yes	no
rug	yes	no
table	yes	no
TV	yes	no

 A. What do you have in your bedroom? Circle *yes* **or** *no.*
B. Write a sentence.

bed	yes	no
chair	yes	no
lamp	yes	no
rug	yes	no
table	yes	no
TV	yes	no

_____

_____

_____

_____

Review

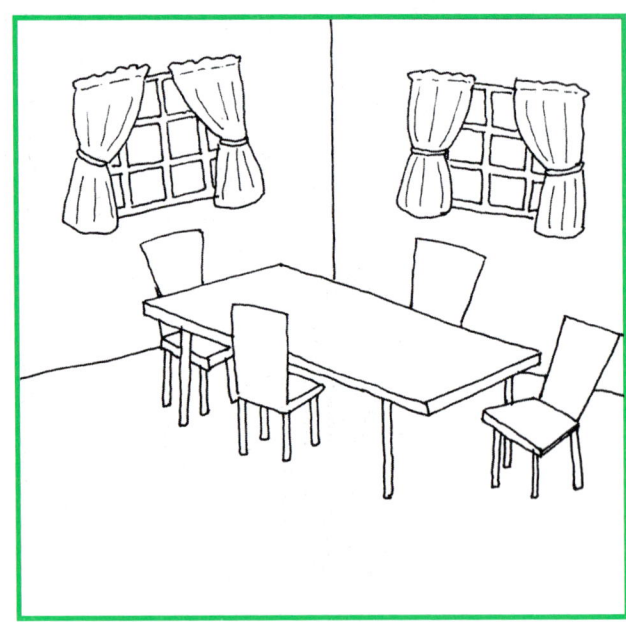

 Read, look, and draw.

1. Draw a clock in the kitchen.
2. Draw a lamp in the bedroom.
3. Draw curtains on the bedroom window.
4. Draw a plant on the dining room table.
5. Draw a rug in the dining room.

 Choose the best word. Check.

1. The refrigerator is in the _____.
2. The tub is in the _____.
3. The night table is in the _____.
4. The sink is in the _____.

☐ living room   ✔ kitchen

☐ kitchen   ☐ bathroom

☐ dining room   ☐ bedroom

☐ kitchen   ☐ living room

Cut-out Activity ✂

Where is it in a house?
Cut and glue. Work with a partner.

Where are the beds?

They're in the bedroom.

bedroom

bathroom

living room

kitchen

dining room

beds	cabinets	chairs	clock	dresser	lamp
mirror	picture	refrigerator	rug	shelves	shower
sink	sofa	stove	table	tub	TV

Students glue the words in the rooms where the items are found in their homes.
Then they work with a partner to ask and answer questions *(Where is. . .?/*
Where are. . .?) about the location of the items.

Draw and color.

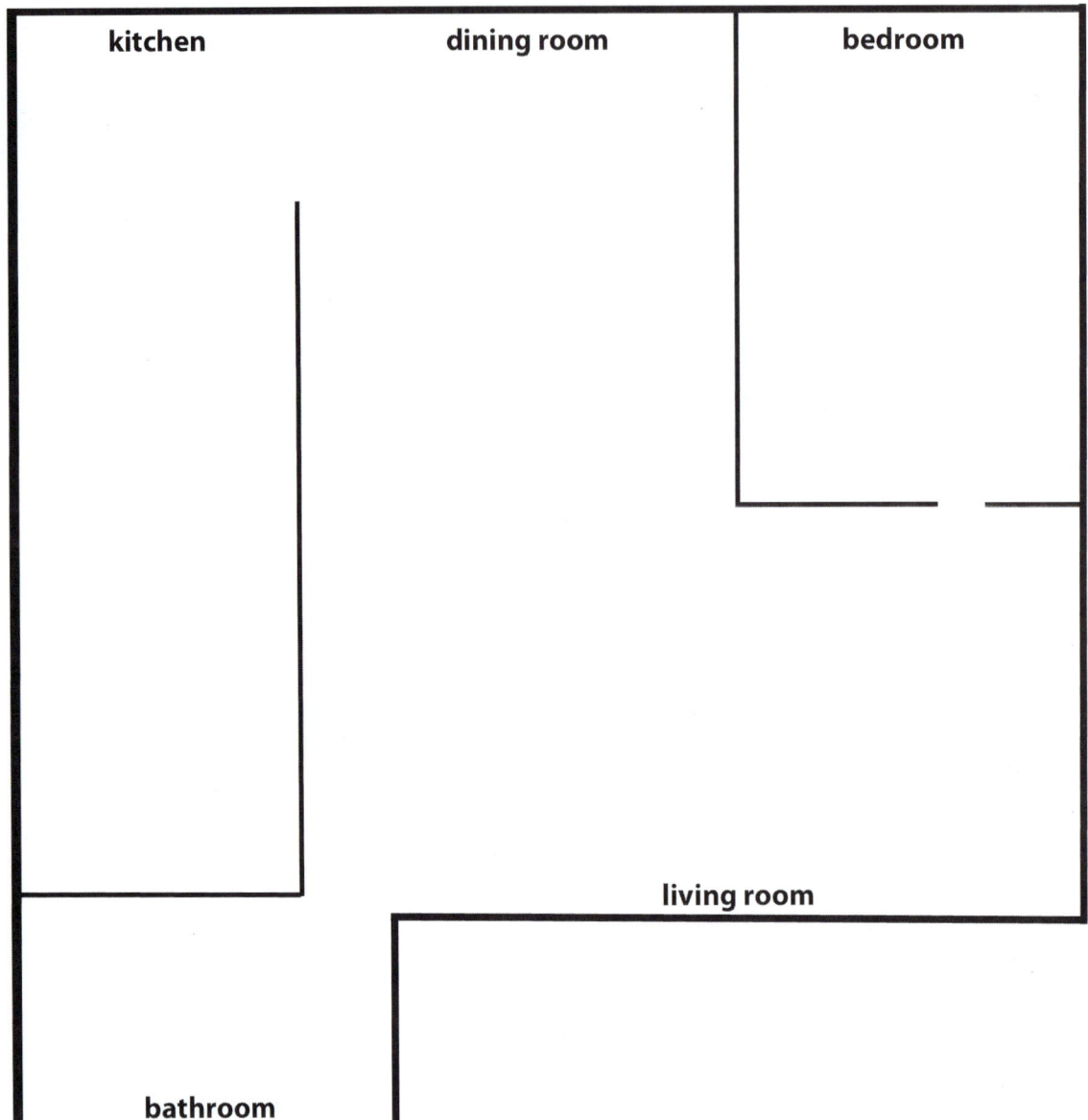

kitchen   dining room   bedroom

living room

bathroom

Students draw and color where things are in their homes.

4 My Town

TRACK 12

1 **Listen and write. Circle the picture.**

Shopping Downtown

I love to go downtown.
There's so much to see.

Daddy, there's a _____ .

Let's get some _____ for me!

I love to go downtown.
There's so much to see.
Please, please, please,
     Daddy, please!

I love to go downtown.
There's so much to see.

Mommy, there's a _____ .

Let's get a _____ for me!

I love to go downtown.
There's so much to see.
Please, please, please,
     Mommy, please!

Please, Daddy, please!
Mommy, please!

Write. Use words from the box.

Our Neighborhood

between	in	next to	on the corner

1. The grocery store is _____ the bookstore and the video store.

2. The toy store is _____ the movie theater.

3. The restaurant is _____ the fire station.

4. There is a computer store _____.

5. There is a shoe store _____ our neighborhood.

6. There is a video store _____.

Grammar

Is there a restaurant on Back Street?	**Yes, there is.** **No, there isn't.**
Are there two video stores on Park Street?	**Yes, there are.** **No, there aren't.**

3 **Write *Yes, there is* or *No, there isn't*.**

1. Is there a police station on Spring Street? _____

2. Is there a video store next to the police station? _____

3. Is there a bus station on the corner? _____

4 **Write *Yes, there are* or *No, there aren't*.**

1. Are there any bookstores on Winter Street? _____

2. Are there two toy stores on Winter Street? _____

3. Are there two restaurants between the grocery store and the fire station?

_____

5 **Write *Is there* or *Are there*. Ask and answer.**

1. _____ any restaurants on Back Street?

2. _____ a supermarket on Main Street?

3. _____ any banks on Main Street?

4. _____ a toy store on Back Street?

5. _____ a music store on Main Street?

6 **Write. Use words from the box.**

| computer store | fire station | restaurant | shoe store | toy store |

1. You can buy  at the _____.

2. You can shop for a  at the _____.

3. You can buy  at the _____.

4. You can see a  at the _____.

5. You can eat  at the _____.

34

Read. Write the missing letters.

What is it?

1. You can buy a bus ticket here.
2. You can buy shoes here.
3. You can mail a letter here.
4. You can get money here.
5. You can buy music here.

6. You can buy toys here.
7. You can buy videos here.
8. You can eat food here.
9. You can try out computers here.

10.

1. b u s   s t a t i o n
2. ___ ___ ___ e ___ ___ ___ ___ ___
3. ___ o ___ ___ ___ ___ ___ ___ ___ ___
4. ___ a ___ ___
5. ___ u ___ ___ ___ ___ ___ ___ ___
6. ___ ___ y ___ ___ ___ ___ ___
7. v ___ ___ ___ ___ ___ ___ ___ ___
8. ___ ___ ___ ___ ___ ___ ___ ___ ___
9. ___ ___ ___ ___ ___ ___ ___ ___ ___ ___ ___

10. Where can you buy books? _____

 Choose two places. Draw and color. Write the names.

bank

fire station

music store

restaurant

shoe store

supermarket

toy store

video store

9 **Listen. Check *yes* or *no*.**

yes   no

1. There's a bank on the corner of Pine Street and River Road.

2. The shoe store is on Martin Street, next to the bus station.

3. The post office is on 16th Street, near the hospital.

4. The restaurant is on Park Road, between the computer store and the music store.

5. Mack's new house is the one with the blue door, on the corner.

6. There's a toy store on the corner of Oak Street and Bennett Street.

10 **Listen and circle. Connect the letters.**

My City Kitty

My curious kitty likes the city.
She plays downtown all day.
Is she here in the (music)/ **computer** store?
(Meow, meow) Here kitty, kitty!

My curious kitty likes the city.
She plays downtown all day.
Is she here in the **grocery / video** store?
(Meow, meow) Here kitty, kitty!

My curious kitty likes the city.
She plays downtown all day.
Is she here in the **bank / restaurant**?
(Meow, meow) Here kitty, kitty!

Places Around the World

What is it?

Where is it?

It's a tower.

In Seoul, Korea.

11 **Read *Places Around the World*. Draw lines to match *where* it is to *what* it is.**

1. Kenya
(in Africa)

2. Mexico
(in North America)

3. Japan
(in Asia)

4. Korea
(in Asia)

12 **What amazing place is in your town or city? Write.**

_____

_____

Review

13 **Check** *next to,* *between,* **or** *on the corner.* **Write.**

1. The fire station is _____ the shoe store.

   ☐ next to   ☐ between   ☐ on the corner

2. The bank is _____.

   ☐ next to   ☐ between   ☐ on the corner

3. The shoe store is _____ the bank and the fire station.

   ☐ next to   ☐ between   ☐ on the corner

14 **Look at 13. Write** *Yes, there is* **or** *No, there isn't.*

1. Is there a police station next to the movie theater?

   _____

2. Is there a supermarket between the police station and the movie theater?

   _____

3. Is there a fire station on the corner?

   _____

15 **Answer the questions.**

1. Where can you get money? _____

2. Where can you buy food? _____

Cut-out Activity ✂ - - - - - - - - - - - - -

A. Cut and glue.
B. Work with a partner.

Is there a computer store on Water Street?

Yes, there is. It's on the corner next to the movie theater.

	computer store
	movie theater
bank	

Water Street

supermarket
fire station
post office

First Street — — — — — — — — — — — —

train station			hospital

bookstore	bus station	police station	restaurant
school	shoe store	toy store	video store

Students work in pairs. Student 1 places or glues the cutouts to complete the map and then hides the map from Student 2. Student 2 tries to duplicate the map by asking questions.

5 My Busy Family

1 Listen and write. Draw lines to match.

Working Hard!

Monday, Tuesday, Wednesday,
   Thursday, Friday, too.
We work hard all week long.
We're busy, busy, busy!

My _____'s a chef—
   he cooks food.
He's busy!

My _____'s a nurse—
   she gives shots.
She's busy!

My _____ makes toy robots.
He's busy!

My _____ studies hard in school.
She's busy!

Monday, Tuesday, Wednesday,
   Thursday, Friday, too.
We work hard all week long.
We're busy, busy, busy!

Write. Use words from the box.

factory	hospital	lab
restaurant	school	shop

1. A factory worker works in a _____.

2. A teacher works in a _____.

3. A chef works in a _____.

4. A nurse works in a _____.

5. A shopkeeper works in a _____.

6. A scientist works in a _____.

Grammar

am	I **am** a teacher.	
is	He **is** a student.	She **is** a student.
are	You **are** a student.	They **are** students.

3 **Write *am, is,* or *are*.**

1. She _____ a ballet dancer.

2. I _____ a musician.

3. They _____ actors.

4. She _____ a firefighter.

5. You _____ a student.

6. He _____ a pilot.

Grammar

I	I **work** in a shop.	
he/she	He **works** in a shop.	She **works** in a shop.
you/they	You **work** in a shop.	They **work** in a shop.

4 **Write *work* or *works*.**

1. They _____ in a lab.

2. I _____ in a hospital.

3. He _____ in a factory.

4. You _____ in a school.

5. She _____ in a restaurant.

6. I _____ in a theater.

 Write. Use words from the box.

1. A nurse _____.
2. A soccer player _____.
3. A pilot _____.
4. An actor _____.
5. A chef _____.

cooks food
flies planes
gives shots
makes movies
plays soccer

 Write.

1. What does she do?

   She makes music.

2. What does he do?

   _____

3. What does he do?

   _____

4. What does he do?

   _____

44

7 Do the puzzle.

Across →

1. He works in a shop.
2. She flies planes.
3. He gives shots.
4. She works in a restaurant.

Down ↓

5. She makes music.
6. He makes movies.
7. She does experiments.
8. He puts out fires.

1. s h o p k e e p e r

8 What does your family do? Draw and color. Write.

My _____ is _____. He _____.

My _____ is _____. She _____.

9 Listen and circle.

1. Mrs. Lopez is a **doctor / dancer**.

2. Carol's uncle is an **actor / artist**.

3. Mark's father is a **teacher / scientist**.

4. Mr. Marimoto is a **chef / soccer player**.

5. Linda's mom is a **factory worker / housewife**.

6. Iris wants to be a **photographer / musician**.

10 Listen and write. Use words from the box. Write another verse.

When I Grow Up

When I grow up, when I grow up,

  I want to _____.

I want to be a _____, just like my mom.

When I grow up, when I grow up,

  I want to _____.

I want to be a _____, just like my dad.

When I grow up, when I grow up,

  I want to _____.

I want to be a _____, just like my aunt.

◆   ◆   ◆

When I grow up, when I grow up,

  I want to _____.

I want to be a _____, just like my _____.

chef
cook good food
fly a plane
pilot
teacher
work in a school

Busy Friends

 Read *Busy Friends*. Draw lines to match.

1. Lee plays the piano.

2. Khalid plays soccer.

3. José paints pictures.

4. Yoko goes to the movies.

5. Linda takes pictures.

6. Pat takes dancing lessons.

a. She wants to be a photographer.

b. He wants to be an artist.

c. She wants to be a ballet dancer.

d. He wants to be a musician.

e. She wants to be an actor.

f. He wants to be a soccer player.

 Are you busy after school? Check the boxes. Write two sentences.

_____

_____

Review

13 **Check *yes* or *no*. Write.**

1. He's an actor.

   ☐ Yes, he is.   ☑ No, he's a _____ *doctor* _____.

2. She's a teacher.

   ☐ Yes, she is.   ☐ No, she's a _____.

3. She's a ballet dancer.

   ☐ Yes, she is.   ☐ No, she's a _____.

4. He's a firefighter.

   ☐ Yes, he is.   ☐ No, he's a _____.

5. She's a scientist.

   ☐ Yes, she is.   ☐ No, she's a _____.

6. He's a factory worker.

   ☐ Yes, he is.   ☐ No, he's a _____.

Cut-out Activity

A. Cut out. Match.
B. Work with a partner. Talk about people and their jobs.

What does a chef do?

A chef cooks food.

A CHEF	cooks food
A TEACHER	dances in a theater
A FACTORY WORKER	does experiments
A SHOPKEEPER	flies planes
A FIREFIGHTER	helps people get well
A DOCTOR	makes movies
A MUSICIAN	makes music
A SCIENTIST	makes toys
AN ACTOR	plays soccer
A BALLET DANCER	puts out fires
A SOCCER PLAYER	works in a school
A PILOT	works in a shop

Students work with partners to match the people with their jobs. They take turns asking and answering questions about the people and what they do. Students can also use both sets of strips to play a match game. They place all strips face down in two piles (people/ what they do) and take turns turning over a strip from each pile to make a match. A student who finds a match gets a second turn. They continue until all strips are matched.

6 Every Day

1 **Listen and write. Use words from the box.**

eight	nine	one	six

From Morning to Night

Tick tock, it's _____ o'clock,

_____ o'clock in the morning.

_____ o'clock is time for school.

Hear the bell? That's my warning!

Now it's _____ o'clock, time for lunch,

_____ in the afternoon.

I know that it's lunchtime when I hear this tune.

It's _____ o'clock, homework time,

_____ o'clock in the evening.

Now I get my homework done.

I really like my reading.

Tick tock, it's _____ o'clock.

It's _____ o'clock at night—

   time to go to bed, time to turn out the light.

From the morning to the afternoon,

   in the evening and at night,

I do all the things I do when the time is right.

Look and write. Use number words.

1. It's _____
o'clock.

2. It's _____
o'clock.

3. It's _____
o'clock.

4. It's _____
o'clock.

5. It's _____
o'clock.

6. It's _____
o'clock.

7. It's _____
o'clock.

8. It's _____
o'clock.

9. It's _____
o'clock.

When do you do homework?	I do homework **in the afternoon**.
What do you do after dinner?	I **watch TV**.

 **Write *When* or *What*.**

1. _____When_____ does he get dressed?
   He gets dressed in the morning.

2. _____ do they do after school?
   They play ball after school.

3. _____ does he eat dinner?
   He eats dinner in the evening.

4. _____ does she do after dinner?
   She does homework after dinner.

5. _____ does he do at night?
   He goes to bed at night.

 Write. Use words from the box.

nine o'clock	one o'clock
seven o'clock	three o'clock

1. I get dressed at _____ in the morning.

2. He goes to bed at _____ at night.

3. They eat lunch at _____ in the afternoon.

4. They walk home from school at _____ in the afternoon.

5 Answer the questions.

1. What does Mario do in the morning?

_____

2. What does Mario do in the afternoon?

_____

3. What does Mario do at night?

_____

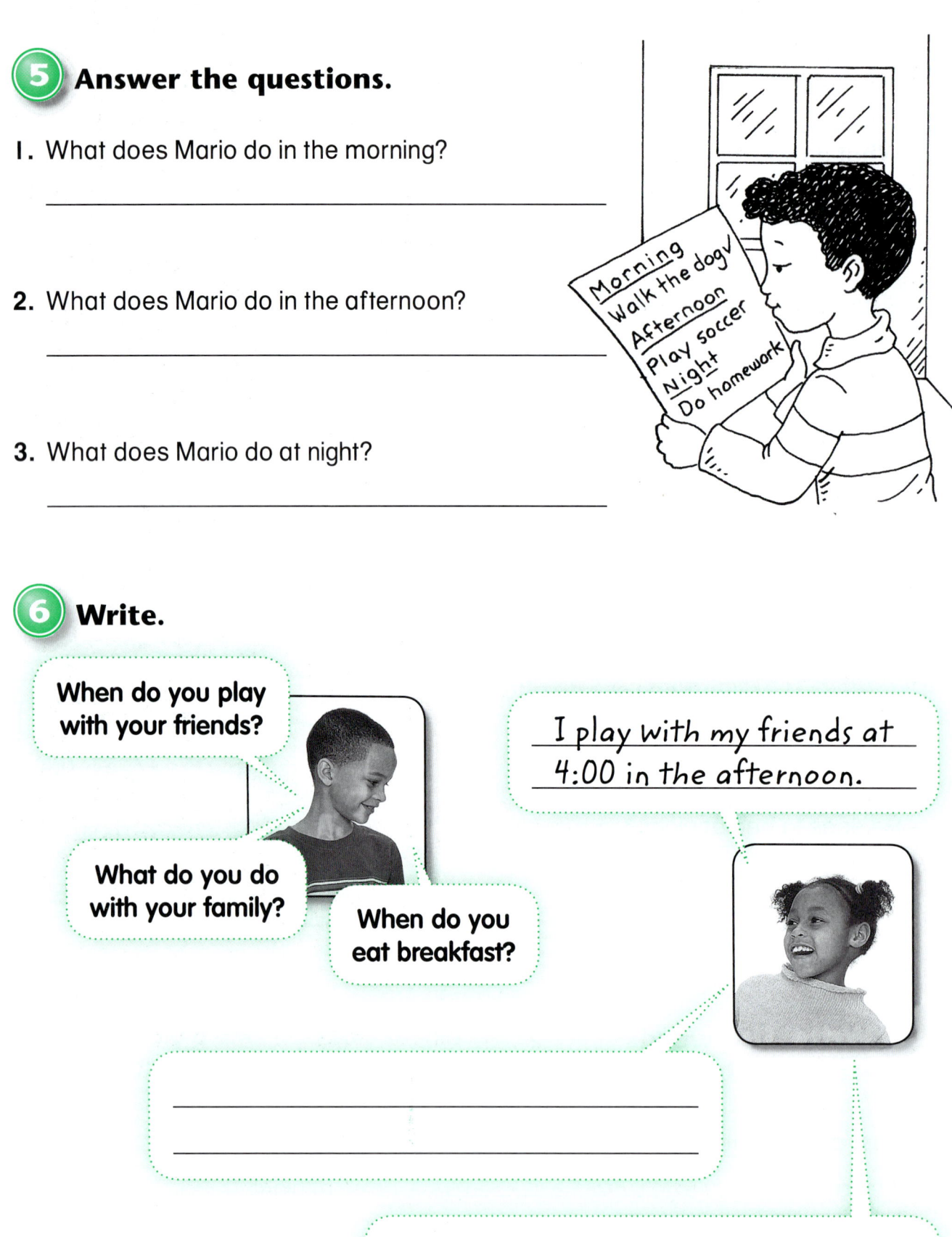

Morning
Walk the dog ✓
Afternoon
Play soccer
Night
Do homework

6 Write.

When do you play
with your friends?

I play with my friends at
4:00 in the afternoon.

What do you do
with your family?

When do you
eat breakfast?

_____
_____

_____
_____

7 **Circle the best words in the box.**

I | wake up / go to bed | in the morning

when the | moon / sun | shines so bright,

I | ride my bike / eat breakfast | in the afternoon,

then I | go to school / go to bed | at night!

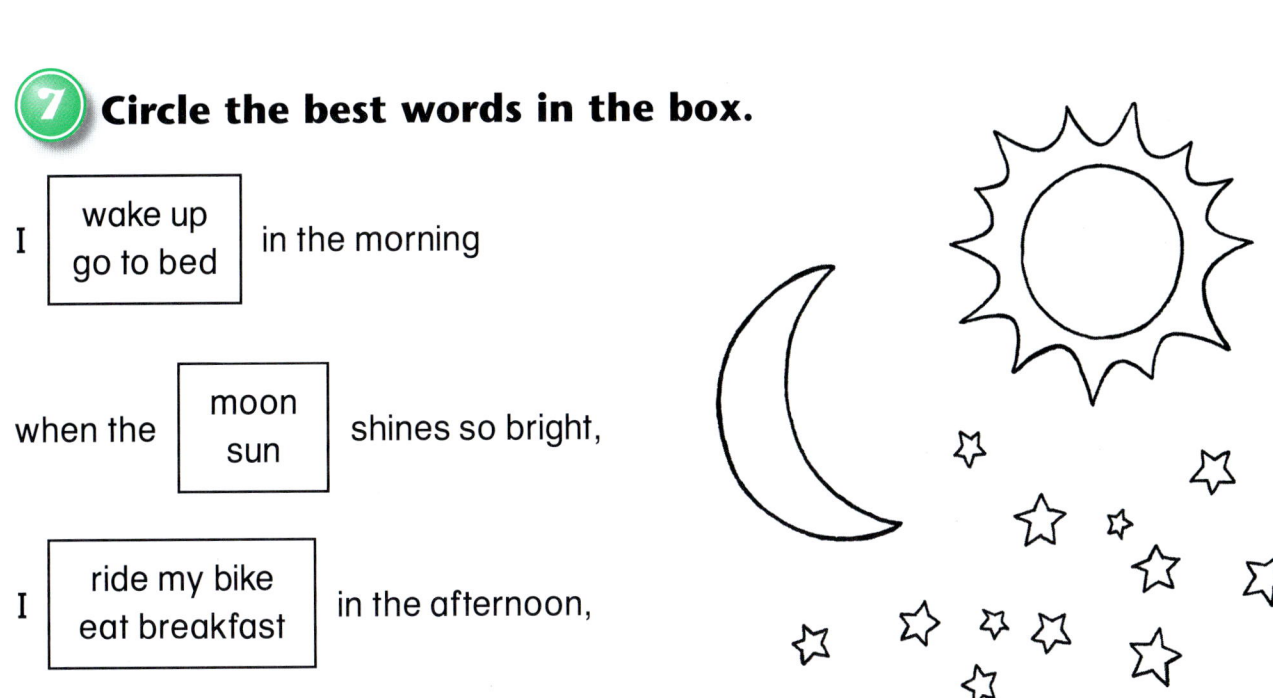

8 **What do you do in the afternoon? Write. Draw and color.**

I _____ in the afternoon.

9 **Listen and match. Draw lines.**

1. Dan feeds his dog   **a.** in the afternoon.

2. They're going to the park   **b.** at 8:00.

3. They go to bed   **c.** every day.

4. Lucy does her homework   **d.** at 4:00.

5. He and his friends ride bikes   **e.** in the morning.

10 **Listen. Write.**

Hurry, Hurry!

Oh, no! It's really late!

Wash your  _____ and get your _____!

Hurry, hurry! Time for school!

Oh, no! It's really late!

Eat your _____ and brush your _____!

Hurry, hurry! Time for school!

Oh, no! It's really late!

Get your _____ and get your _____!

Hurry, hurry! Time for school!

No, Mom. It isn't late!

Look at the  _____ on the wall!

It's Sunday—no school at all!

Perfect Penny

11 **Read _Perfect Penny_. Check the boxes.**

1. At 7:00, Penny _____.

   ☐ covers her hair

   ☐ eats her breakfast

   ☐ feeds her cat

2. At 7:15, Penny _____.

   ☐ gets dressed

   ☐ goes to school

   ☐ takes a bath

3. At 7:30, Penny _____.

   ☐ wakes up

   ☐ does her homework

   ☐ gets dressed

4. At 7:45, Penny _____.

   ☐ is ready to leave the bathroom

   ☐ goes to bed

   ☐ takes a bath

12 **What happens next? What do you think Penny does at 8:00? Write.**

_____

_____

13 **What is Penny's favorite color? How do you know? Write.**

_____

_____

Review

 Look at the clock. Write the time. Use words from the box.

1. When does she get dressed?

   She gets dressed at _____.

2. When does he eat lunch?

   He eats lunch at _____.

3. When does she go to bed?

   She goes to bed at _____.

| nine o'clock |
| one o'clock |
| seven o'clock |

15 **Answer the questions.**

1. What do you do in the morning?

   _____

2. What do you do at school?

   _____

3. What do you do in the afternoon?

   _____

Cut-out Activity ✂----

When do you eat breakfast?

I eat breakfast at seven o'clock in the morning.

Cut and glue. Work with a partner.

In the morning	
at seven o'clock	
at eight o'clock	
at nine o'clock	
In the afternoon	
at one o'clock	
at four o'clock	
In the evening	
at six o'clock	
at seven o'clock	
at nine o'clock	

do homework	eat breakfast	eat dinner
eat lunch	get dressed	get up
go to bed	go to school	play with friends
ride a bike	take a bath	watch TV

Students complete the chart about themselves. They place or glue activity strips next to the time. Then they work in pairs to ask and answer questions about their day. Students should answer with an exact time and say *in the morning/afternoon/evening*. Students can also add other activities.

Favorite Foods

1 **Listen and write. Use words from the box. Trace and color.**

dessert	fruit juices
meat	vegetables

Yum! Yum!

Yum, yum!
I like orange juice and apple juice.
I like _____.
How about you?

I like carrots and tomatoes.
I like _____.

I like chicken and hamburgers.
I like all kinds of _____.
Yum, yum! Yum, yum!

I like ice cream and chocolate cake.
I like _____.
I like all kinds of different food.
I like to eat.

Yum, yum! Yum, yum!
Yum, yum! Yum, yum!

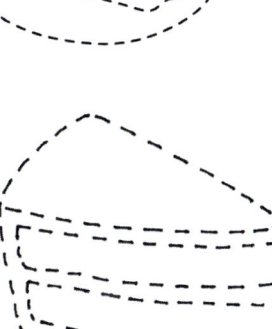

2 Write. Use words from the box.

1. I have _____ apple.

2. Soon-Jin has _____ cake.

3. Joe has _____ carrot.

4. Lok has _____ chicken.

5. Vita has _____ hamburger.

6. Benito has _____ ice cream.

7. Karen has _____ tomato.

8. Lee has _____ orange.

a
an
some

3 Look at the pictures. Draw lines to match.

a

an

some

Do	you	**like** meat?	Yes,	I	**do**.	I	**like** ham and steak.
			No,	I	**don't**.	I	**don't like** meat.
Does	he / she	**like** meat?	Yes,	he / she	**does**.	He / She	**likes** steak.
			No,	he / she	**doesn't**.	He / She	**doesn't like** meat.

4 **Look at the chart. Write.**

Does Mary like it?	
Yes	**No**

1. Does Mary like chicken?

   Yes, she does.

2. Does she like strawberries?

   _____

3. Does she like tortilla chips and salsa?

   _____

4. Does she like green beans?

   _____

5. Does Mary like fish?

   _____

6. Does she like hamburgers?

   _____

7. Does she like cheese and crackers?

   _____

8. Does she like mangoes?

   _____

5 **What foods do you like?**

_____

_____

_____

Look and write. Use *like, likes, don't like,* and *doesn't like*.

1. Julia _____ doesn't like _____ cookies.

2. I _____ grapes.

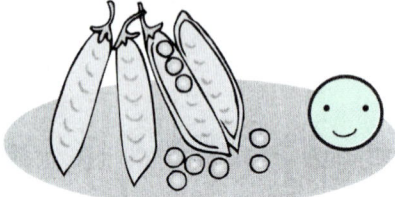

3. José _____ peas.

4. I _____ pineapple.

5. Ricky _____ peppers.

6. I _____ chocolate cake.

7. Hilda _____ cheese.

7 Write questions.

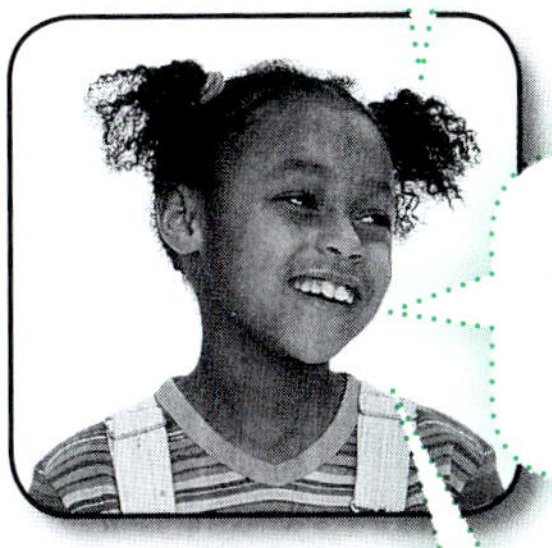

1. ______________________
______________ chicken?

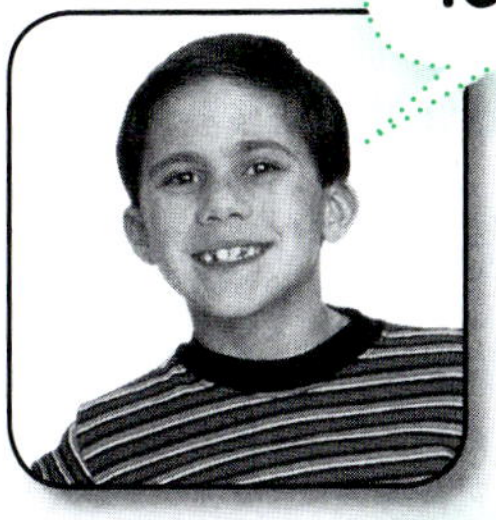

Yes, I do.

2. ______________________
______________ shrimp?

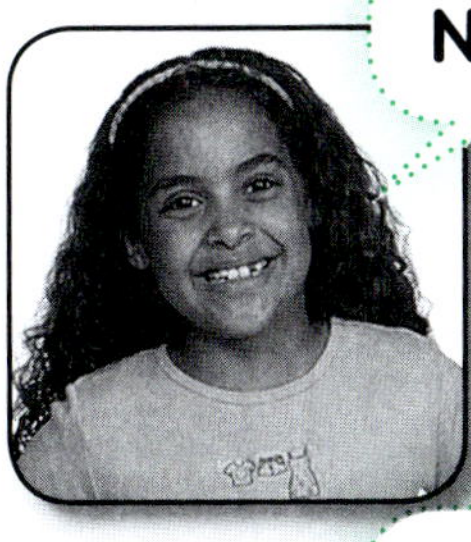

No, she doesn't.

3. ______________________
______________ cabbage?

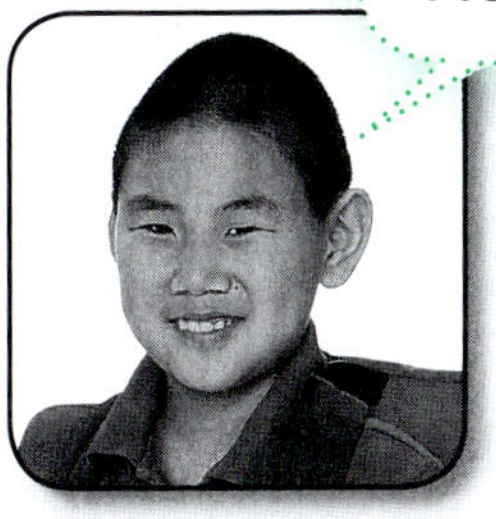

No, I don't.

8 What's in the shopping cart? Find seven words. Circle them.

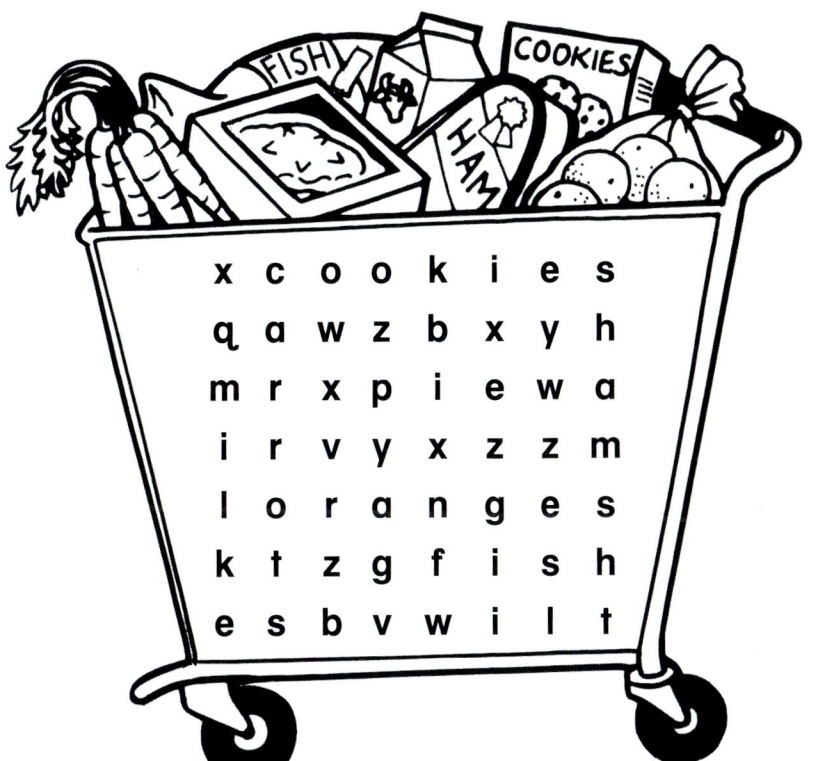

FISH
COOKIES
HAM
x c o o k i e s
q a w z b x y h
m r x p i e w a
i r v y x z z m
l o r a n g e s
k t z g f i s h
e s b v w i l t

TRACK 22

9 Listen. Check *true* or *false*.

	true	false
1. The restaurant has chicken and potatoes.	☐	☐
2. She doesn't like chocolate ice cream.	☐	☐
3. He wants to drink some orange juice.	☐	☐
4. She likes shrimp and cabbage.	☐	☐
5. They want cereal with milk for breakfast.	☐	☐

TRACK 23

10 Listen and write. Use words from the box.

bread	cereal	cheese	eggs	meats	muffins

Bobby's Big Breakfast

Here we are at the breakfast buffet.
Come on, Bobby, don't take all day!

Gee, I don't know what to do.

I want bacon and _____ and _____, too!

We're waiting and waiting at the breakfast buffet.
Come on, Bobby, don't take all day!

Gee, I don't know what to do.

I want _____ and jam and _____, too!

We're waiting and waiting at the breakfast buffet.
Come on, Bobby, don't take all day!

Gee, I don't know what to do.

I want fruit and _____ and cold _____, too!

Food Comes from Everywhere

11 **Read *Food Comes from Everywhere*. Check *yes* or *no*.**

	yes	no
1. Bread comes from wheat.	☐	☐
2. Mussels come from trees.	☐	☐
3. Cheese comes from cows.	☐	☐
4. Fish come from oceans and rivers.	☐	☐
5. Pine nuts come from chickens.	☐	☐
6. Lemons come from trees.	☐	☐
7. Noodles come from cows.	☐	☐
8. Eggs come from chickens.	☐	☐

12 **What is your favorite food? Where does it come from? Write.**

My favorite food is spaghetti.
Spaghetti comes from wheat.

My favorite food is _____.

_____ comes from _____.

Review

13 **Color the foods. Point and say. Draw lines to match.**

apple

banana

cake

cheese

chicken

lemonade

peas

pie

shrimp

tomato

14 **Answer the questions.**

1. Do you like cabbage? _____, _____.

2. Do you like ice cream? _____, _____.

3. Do you like nuts? _____, _____.

4. Do you like onions? _____, _____.

5. What do you want to eat and drink? _____

Cut-out Activity ✂ -------------------

A. **Cut and glue. Check (✔)** *like* **or (x)** *don't like.*

B. **Work with a partner. Talk about what you like and don't like.**

Do you like trout?

No, I don't.

Foods from animals

Foods from plants and trees

Foods from water

---

apples ☐	bananas ☐	bread ☐	eggs ☐	green beans ☐
hamburgers ☐	ice cream ☐	lemons ☐	mangoes ☐	pine nuts ☐
popcorn ☐	shrimp ☐	steak ☐	tortilla chips ☐	trout ☐

Students glue foods in the correct categories and mark what they like and don't like. Then students work with a partner to ask and answer questions with *Yes, I do* or *No, I don't.*

Fun at the Zoo

z

 **1** TRACK 24 **Listen. Write numbers and words.**

At the Zoo

What do you want to see today
    when we go to the zoo?
I want to see the (1), (2), and (3)!

_____

What do you want to see today
    when we go to the zoo?
I want to see the (4), (5), and (6), too!

What do you want to see today
    when we go to the zoo?
Animals from around the world
    that say more than moo!
Let's go to the zoo!

_____

I want to see (7) and (8)
    and (9) and monkeys
    and cheetahs and hippos,
    snakes and polar bears, too.
When we go to the zoo….
Let's go to the zoo!

_____

(1) elephants
_____

_____

_____

_____

_____

_____

b
Unit 8

71

2 Write. Use words from the box.

feathers	mouth	neck	tail	teeth

1. A hippo is short.

   Its _____ is big.

2. A polar bear is big.

   Its _____ is short.

3. A giraffe is tall.

   Its _____ is long.

4. A lion is strong.

   Its _____ are sharp.

5. Peacocks are small.

   Their _____ are soft.

Can a monkey climb a tree?	Yes, it **can**.	
Can a monkey catch seals?	No, it **can't**.	
		can't = cannot
Can crocodiles swim fast?	Yes, they **can**.	
Can crocodiles climb trees?	No, they **can't**.	

 Circle *can* or *can't*.

1. Giraffes **can** **can't** eat the leaves of tall trees.

2. Cheetahs **can** **can't** run very fast.

3. Snakes **can** **can't** jump high.

4. Monkeys **can** **can't** swing from trees.

5. Elephants **can** **can't** lift heavy things.

4 Write *can* or *can't*.

1. A crocodile _____ climb a tree.

2. A kangaroo _____ jump high.

3. An elephant _____ swim fast.

4. A polar bear _____ catch fish.

5. A lion _____ eat with its sharp teeth.

5 Write.

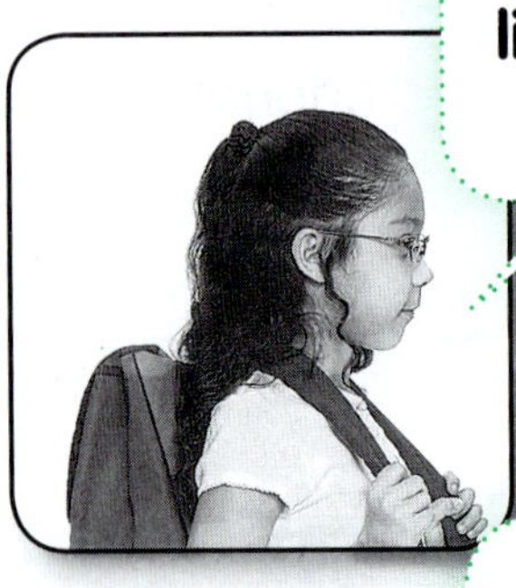

Can an elephant lift things with its trunk?

Yes, it can.

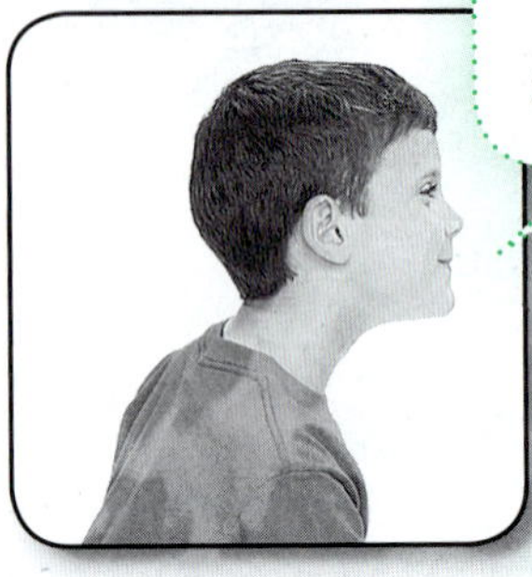

Can giraffes swing from trees?

_____
_____

_____
_____
_____

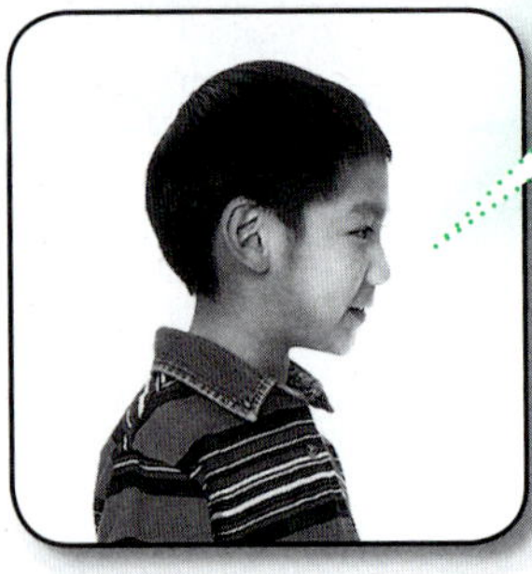

_____
_____

6 Read. Write numbers.

1. This animal doesn't have legs. It can catch and squeeze animals.

2. This animal has a short tail and sharp claws. It can catch seals.

3. This animal has strong legs. It can run very fast.

74

Does a hippo **have** a big mouth?   Yes, it **does**.
Does a hippo **have** a long tail?   No, it **doesn't**.   doesn't = does not

Do lions **have** sharp teeth?   Yes, they **do**.   don't = do not
Do lions **have** long necks?   No, they **don't**.

 Answer the questions.

1. Does a giraffe have a long neck?

   _____

2. Does an elephant have feathers?

   _____

3. Do crocodiles have short legs?

   _____

4. Do peacocks have long trunks?

   _____

8 **A. Draw a new animal.**

**B. Talk about your animal. What does your animal
  have? What doesn't it have?**

TRACK 25

9 **Listen and circle.**

1. a peacock   a hippo   a monkey

2. a polar bear   a cheetah   a kangaroo

3. a snake   a giraffe   an elephant

4. a crocodile   a bird   a snake

5. a dog   a peacock   a cheetah

6. a rabbit   a monkey   a crocodile

TRACK 26

 **10** **Listen and write. Choose words from the boxes. Write each word two times.**

Act Like the Animals

1. I can _____ a tree like a monkey,
   and act like a monkey, too.

   I can _____ a tree like a monkey.
   It's your turn—what about you?

2. I can _____ real fast like a cheetah,
   and act like a cheetah, too.

   I can _____ real fast like a cheetah.
   It's your turn—what about you?

3. I can _____ in the water like a crocodile,
   and act like a crocodile, too.

   I can _____ in the water like a crocodile.
   It's your turn—what about you?

climb   run   squeeze   fly   swim   jump

The Lion and the Rabbit

11 **Read *The Lion and the Rabbit*. Check *yes* or *no*.**

	yes	no
1. King Lion catches Rabbit for his dinner.	☐	☐
2. King Lion takes Rabbit to a deep well.	☐	☐
3. King Lion looks at his reflection in the well.	☐	☐
4. King Lion says, "I am king of this well."	☐	☐
5. Rabbit jumps into the well because he is happy.	☐	☐

12 **What comes next? Check one box. Draw.**

☐ Rabbit eats a carrot.

☐ Rabbit sees a crocodile.

☐ Rabbit jumps high.

☐ Rabbit goes home to rest.

Review

13 **Write. Use words from the box.
Draw lines to the animals.**

| catch seals and fish |
| eat leaves from tall trees |
| jump high |
| lift things with its trunk |

1. An elephant can _____.

2. A polar bear can _____.

3. A kangaroo can _____.

4. A giraffe can _____.

5. A giraffe has _____.

6. A cheetah has _____.

7. A monkey has _____.

8. A kangaroo has _____.

| a long neck |
| big feet |
| long arms |
| strong legs |

Cut-out Activity

A. **Cut and glue.**
B. **Work with a partner. Talk about what animals can and can't do.**

Can cheetahs fly?

No, they can't.

Animals	can	can't
monkeys		
crocodiles		
elephants		
giraffes		
kangaroos		
cheetahs		
polar bears		
snakes		

catch food with claws	climb	eat leaves of tall trees
fly	jump	jump high
lift heavy things	lift things	run fast
run very fast	spread their feathers	squeeze animals
swim	swim fast	swing from trees

Students work in pairs to complete the chart. Students cut out strips with what the
animals can do and can't do and glue them by the animals. Then students ask and answer
questions about the animals **Can monkeys: _____? Yes, they can./No, they can't.**

9 12 Months Make a Year

TRACK 27

1 **Listen and write.**

Twelve Months

Thirty days in September,

_____, June, and November—

Shorter than the rest I hear,

but _____ months make a year.

Most other months have 31 days.

January, _____, and May,

July, August, _____, December.

Twelve months make a year.

February has 28—that's great!

Sometimes _____—

that's fine.

There's one thing that is

always clear.

Twelve months make a year.

Can I help you to remember

from January to December?

One thing never changes here.

Twelve months make a year.

How many months
are there?

Grammar

always	✓✓✓✓✓✓✓
never	

2 **Look. Write *always* or *never*.**

Korea in August

Japan in February

Brazil in January

1. In Japan, he _____ goes swimming in February.

2. In Brazil, I _____ go swimming in January.

3. In Korea, she _____ plays in the snow in August.

4. In Japan, I _____ wear a warm jacket in February.

5. In Brazil, they _____ go snow skiing in January.

6. In Korea, I _____ wear shorts in August.

7. In my country, I _____ finish school in June.

8. In my country, I _____ have picnics in April.

What do you do in May?   We **always** celebrate Cinco de Mayo in May.
We **never** go on vacation in May.

3 **Write about you.**

1. What do you do in December? I always

_____ in December.

2. What do you do in July? I never _____ in July.

3. What do you do in August? I always _____
in August.

4. What do you do in September? I always _____
in September.

Grammar

When **do**	you they	**go** swimming?	When **does**	he she	**go** swimming?

4 **Write a question.**

1. 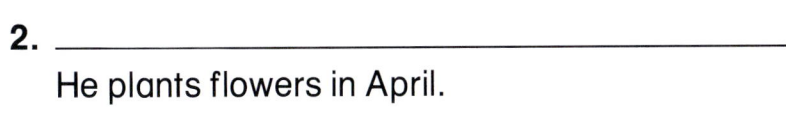   When do they celebrate Christmas?
They celebrate Christmas in December.

2. _____
He plants flowers in April.

3. _____
They start school in February.

4. _____
She has a birthday party in March.

5. _____
They go swimming in January.

 **Write about you.**

1. What do you do in April?

   I _____ in April.

2. What do you do in December?

   I _____ in December.

3. When do you start school?

   I start school in _____.

4. When do you go swimming?

   I go swimming in _____.

Japan in February

6. **Answer the questions.**

1. What does he do?

   _____

   When does he do it?

   _____

2. What do they do?

   _____

   When do they do it?

   _____

Brazil in February

3. What do they do?

   _____

   When do they do it?

   _____

USA in December

 **What month is it? Read and write.**

1. It's between July and September. In some places, it is hot and people go swimming.

   _____

2. It comes right after January. Children in Colombia start school.

   _____

3. It's the month before October. People in Mexico celebrate Independence Day.

   _____

4. It's between December and February. In many places, it is cold and snows a lot.

   _____

 What is your favorite month? Why? Write. Draw.

December is my favorite month. Christmas is in December! _____

_____

9  **Listen and write.**

1. His sister's birthday is in _____.

2 They always have a party in _____.

3. They don't go to the beach in _____.

4. Her favorite month is _____.

5. This year, vacation is in _____.

10 **Listen. Draw lines to match.**

Favorite Months

My favorite month is _____.
Do you want to know why?

I always plant flowers and walk in the rain.
My umbrella keeps me dry.

My favorite month is _____.
Do you want to know why?

I always pick apples and jump in the leaves,
    and eat plenty of pumpkin pie!

My favorite month is _____.
Do you want to know why?

I always play soccer and swim in the lake,
    and fly my kite in the sky.

11 **Write another verse.**

My favorite month is _____. Do you want to know why?

I _____,

    and _____.

My Favorite Month

 Read _My Favorite Month_. Draw lines to match.

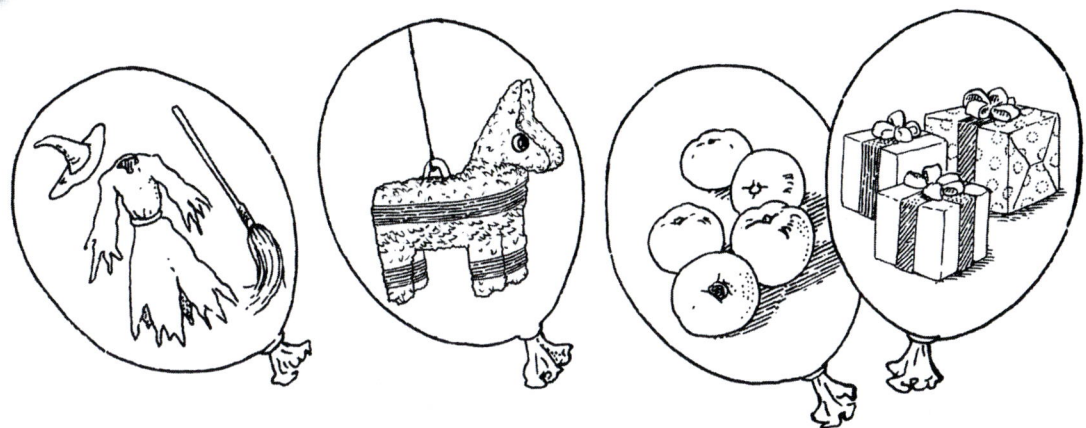

1. Children wear these on this holiday in the United States.

2. Children get these on this special holiday in Korea.

3. Children play games like this on this holiday in Mexico.

4. People have fights with these on this holiday in Spain.

 **Read. Circle.**

1. What holiday in the story do you like?

| Halloween | Las Posadas | La Tomatina | Uhrini nal |

2. What do people like about this holiday?

   a. the tomato fights   **b.** the games, parades, and special food   **c.** the scary costumes   **d.** the nine days of fun

3. This holiday is after May and before October. What is it?

| Las Posadas | La Tomatina | Uhrini nal | Halloween |

Review

14 **Write questions with *what* or *when*.**

1. ___What do people do in April?___

   They plant flowers and trees.

2. ___When do people celebrate Arbor Day?___

   They celebrate Arbor Day in April.

3. _____

   On my birthday, I sing, dance, and eat cake.

4. _____

   My birthday is in October.

5. _____

   We give gifts to each other in December.

6. _____

   In August, we throw tomatoes at each other.

7. _____

   Some people play in the snow.

8. _____

   I start school in March.

15 **Write *always* or *never*.**

1. Children _____ wear costumes on Halloween.

2. In Korea, we _____ celebrate Arbor Day in April.

3. In Mexico, we _____ celebrate Independence Day in June.

4. In Colombia, school _____ starts in February.

Cut-out Activity ✂ - - - - - - - - - - - - - -

A. Cut and glue. Write.
B. Work with a partner.
   Talk about what you
   always do and never do.

What do you do in January?

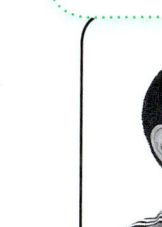

I always wear a warm jacket. I never wear shorts.

Months of the Year	Always	Never
January		
February		
March		
April		
May		
June		
July		
August		
September		
October		
November		
December		

celebrate my birthday	fly a kite	give presents	go on vacation
go skiing	go swimming	have a party	have a picnic
jump in leaves	pick apples	plant flowers	play soccer
start school	wear a costume	wear a warm jacket	wear shorts

Students glue the activities onto the chart and write their own ideas in any
remaining spaces. They ask and answer questions about what they *always*
and *never* do.

1 **Say the words. How many times do you hear *t* as in *table*?**

cat   doctor   elephant   goat   taxi   toes   toy   turtle

2 **Find ten pictures of words with *t* as in *table*. Color the pictures.**

3 **Look at 2. Write ten words with *t* as in *table*.**

robot

1 **Say the words. How many times do you hear *i* as in *six*?**

big   fish   gift   kick   kitchen   milk   picnic   sing

2 **Look at the pictures. Write the words with *i* as in *six* in box 1. Write the words that do not have *i* as in *six* in box 2.**

airplane   cookie   fire truck   fish   kitchen
lion   living room   pink   rice   scissors

fish	lion
1	**2**

1 **Say the words. How many times do you hear the same sound as the c in cat?**

cake   car   catch   cold   cookie   cow   doctor   picnic

2 **Look at the picture and complete the sentence. Say the sentence.**

1. The _____ is walking.

2. That _____ is for the party.

3. The _____ is eating fish.

4. That _____ is new.

5. My uncle is a _____.

6. I like to play _____.

7. I want that big _____.

8. I want the blue _____.

1 **Say the words. How many times do you hear *d* as in *dog*?**

bedroom   dentist   desk   doctor   doll   duck   Friday   red

2 **Buddy the dog wants to find his bone. Find the path using words with *d* as in *dog*.**

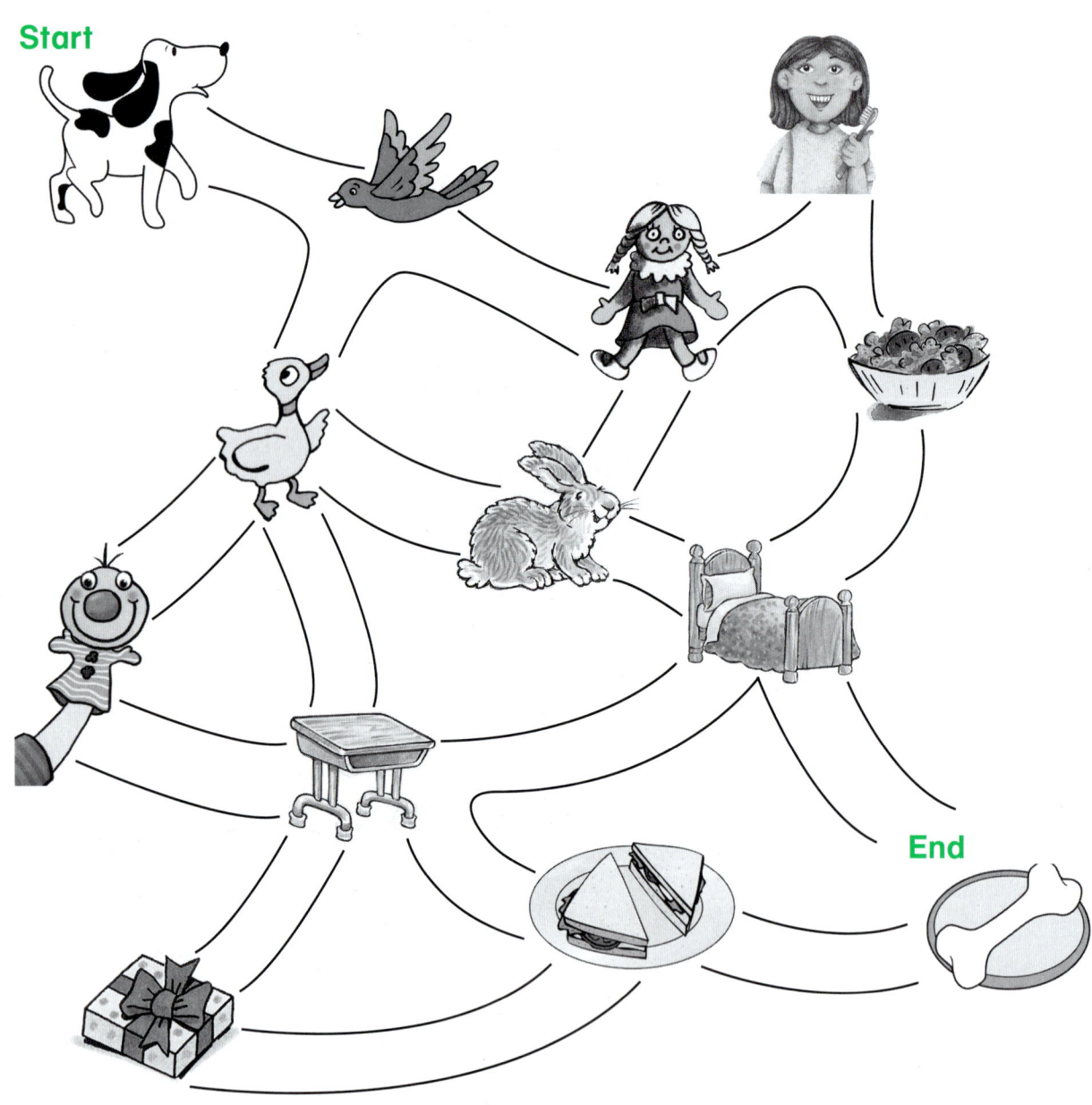

Start

End

Sound and Spelling Handbook   *l* as in *lion*

1 Say the words. How many times do you hear *l* as in *lion*?

school   elephant   family   leg   lemon   little   living room   long

2 Draw an X over the word that doesn't have the same sound as the *l* in *lion*.

1.

2.

3.

4.

3 Look at 2. Write the words with *l* as in *lion*.

_____   _____   _____   _____

_____   _____   _____   _____

1 **Say the words. How many times do you hear *f* as in *foot*?**

family   farmer   feet   firefighter   five   fly   four   giraffe

2 **Do the crossword puzzle. Write the words.**

Down ↓

1.

2.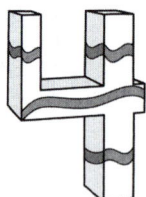

3.

4.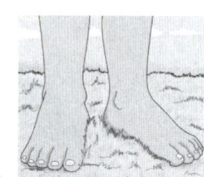

5.

Across →

6.

7.

8.

1 Say the words. How many times do you hear **m** as in **milk**?

arm   bedroom   family   game   jump   marker   milk   monkey

2 Do the crossword puzzle. Write the words.

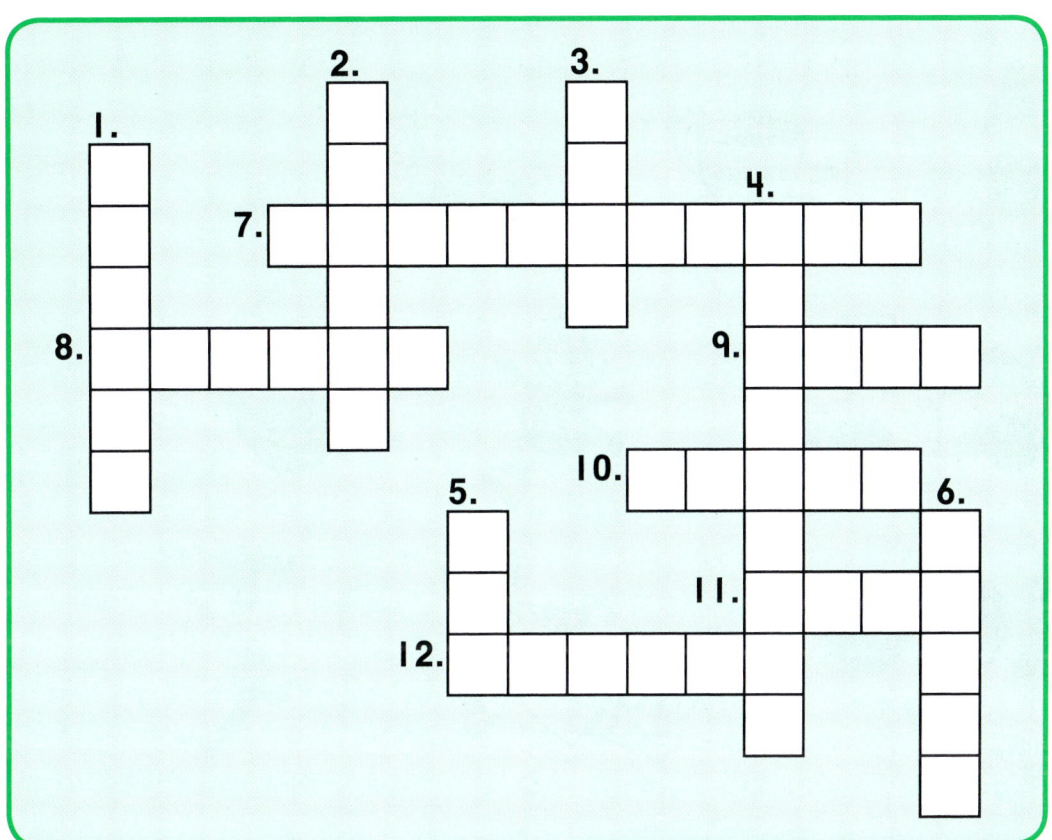

Down ↓

1.

2.

3.

4.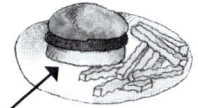

5.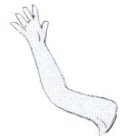

6.

Across →

7.

8.

9.

10.

11.

12.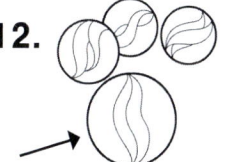

Sound and Spelling Handbook — *u* as in *bus*

1 Say the words. How many times do you hear **u** as in *bus*?

cup duck fun hundred jump puddle run under

2 Draw an X over the word that doesn't have the same sound as the **u** as in *bus*.

1.

2.

3. **100**

4.

3 Look at 2. Write the words that have the same sound as the **u** in *bus*.

_____ _____ _____ _____

_____ _____ _____ _____

Lesson 8: the vowel ***u***

1 **Say the words. How many times do you hear *h* as in *hat*?**

hamburger   he   head   hello   hit   hot   hot dog   hundred

2 **Unscramble and write eight words with *h* as in *hat*. Match.**

oshue   suhb   ihar   rehos   mah   ehad   fhis   nadh   tog hod   durdehn

1. _____

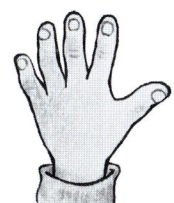

2. _____

3. _____

4. _____

5. _____

6. _____

100

7. _____

8. _____

Move your game piece. Ask and answer.

6.

7. Where is your TV?

8.

9. What do you like to do?

5.

4. What's in your backpack?

3.

2.

1. What does your family like to do?

START

Students can work with partners or by themselves to move their game pieces and answer questions or describe the images. Answers should be in sentence form. Students move ahead if they answer the questions or explain the images correctly. The first person to reach "Finish" wins.

Move your game piece. Ask and answer.

START

1. Where can you shop for food?

2. VIDEO STORE

3.

4. What does a pilot do?

FINISH

20.

19. WINTER ST. TOYS GROCERY STORE

18. When do you feed your pet?

17.

16.

15. What do you want to be?

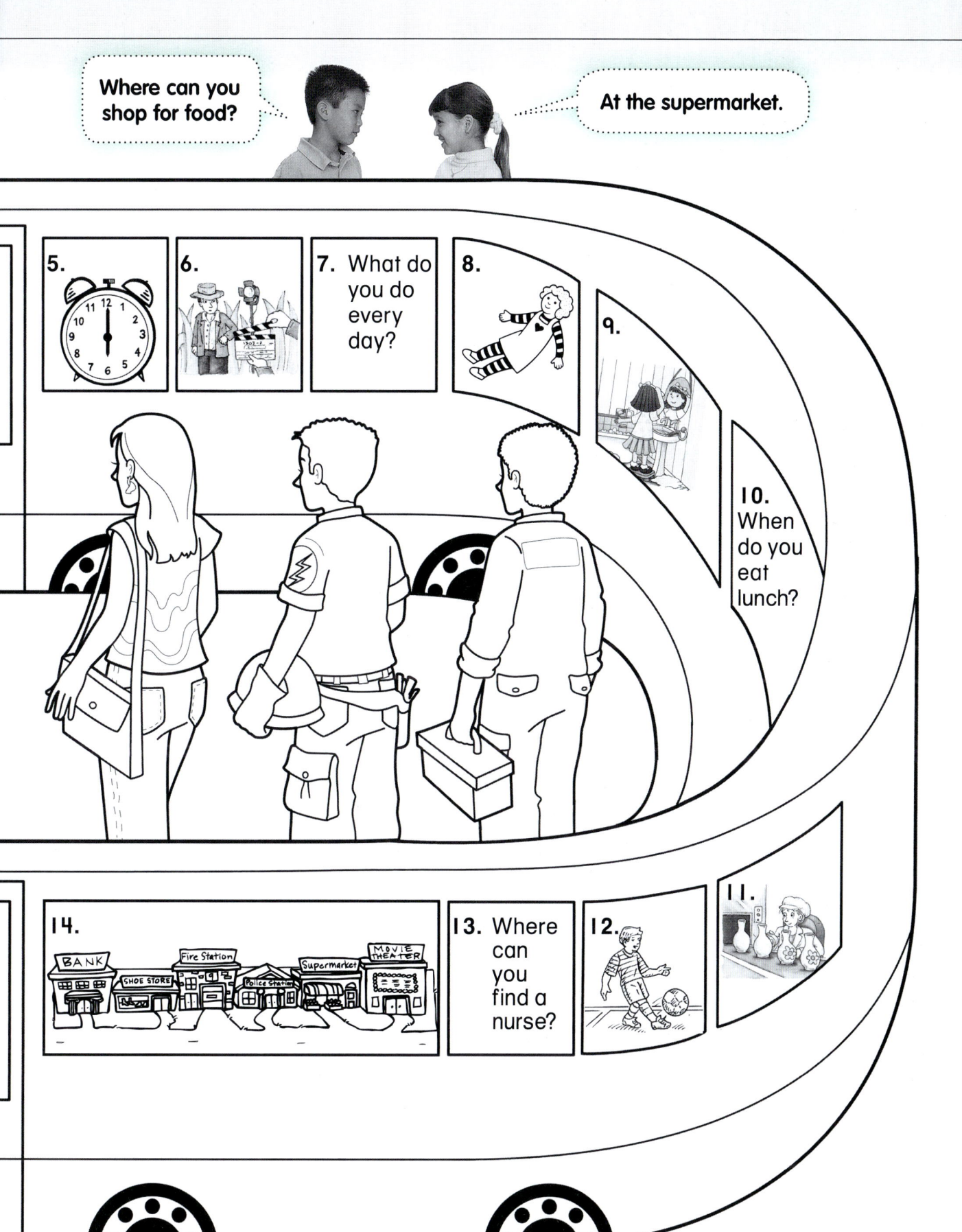

Students can work with partners or by themselves to move their game pieces and answer questions or describe the images. Answers should be in sentence form. Students move ahead if they answer the questions or explain the images correctly. The first person to reach "Finish" wins.

Move your game piece. Ask and answer.

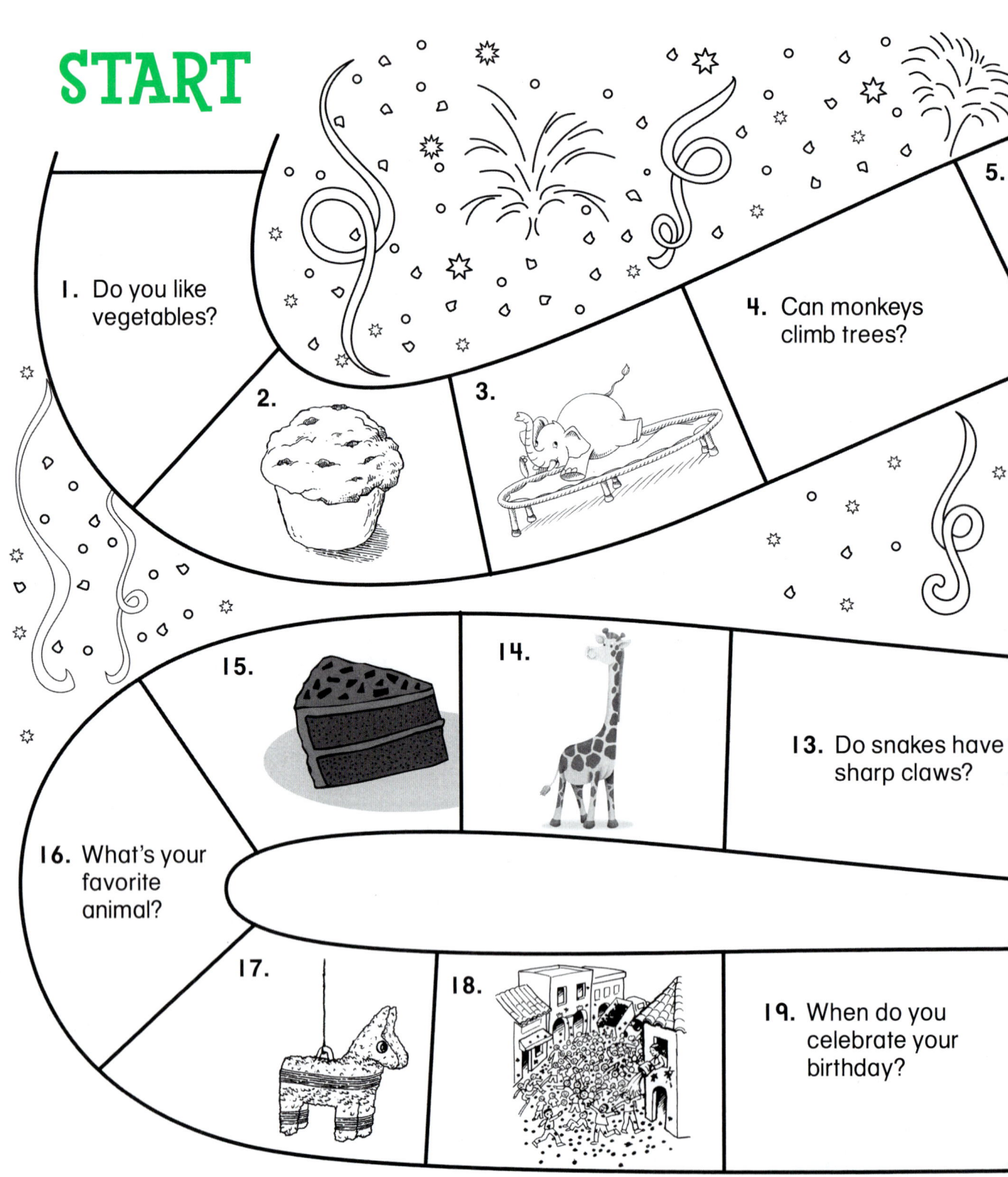

START

1. Do you like vegetables?

2.

3.

4. Can monkeys climb trees?

5.

15.

14.

13. Do snakes have sharp claws?

16. What's your favorite animal?

17.

18.

19. When do you celebrate your birthday?

Grammar and Writing

 Possessive Adjectives: Complete the sentences.

> her   his   its   my   our   their   your

1. Give that notebook to Robert. It's ———————————— notebook.

2. That present is for Linda. It's ———————————— present.

3. Jerry and Bill go to school there. It's ———————————— school.

4. Look at this photo of ———————————— new baby sister! Now I have two!

5. That cat is thirsty. Put some water in ———————————— bowl.

6. We can't watch TV. ———————————— TV is broken.

7. Wow. Is that ———————————— new red bike, Tim?

 Contractions of *Be*: Write.

1. she is ————————————

2. we are ————————————

3. it is ————————————

4. you are ————————————

5. I am ————————————

6. he is ————————————

7. they are ————————————

③ Simple Present: Circle the correct verb.

1. Lucy   **get / gets**   up at 7:00 in the morning.

2. Ice cream   **are / is**   cold.

3. We   **like / likes**   pizza.

4. I   **play / plays**   soccer with my friends.

5. He   **have / has**   a new backpack.

6. They   **eat / eats**   lunch at 1:30.

4 **Simple Present:** Complete the sentences. Use the correct form.

| brush | climb | draw | jump | like | ride |

1. I _____ my teeth after breakfast every day.

2. Our cat _____ the big tree in front of our house.

3. Jenny always _____ pictures of animals.

4. We _____ rope every afternoon.

5. Mark _____ oranges and bananas.

6. They _____ their bikes to school.

5 **Present Progressive:** What are they doing? Write sentences.

1. He _____.
fly / kite

2. They _____.
erase / board

3. I _____.
plant / flowers

4. We _____.
eat / breakfast

6 **Word Order with Adjectives:** Unscramble the sentences.

1. cutting / is / paper / red / she

_____

2. desk / is / next to / the / brown / window / the

_____

3. bedroom / is / her / little

_____

4. is / Frank / a / reading / book / dinosaurs / good / about

_____

5. Marilyn / busy / today / is

_____

6. skateboard / is / that / new

_____

7 **Object Pronouns:** Write.

| her | him | it | me | them | us | you | your |

_____   _____   _____   _____

_____   _____   _____   _____